DARE
TO BE
GREAT

SHANEEN CLARKE

DARE TO BE GREAT
Copyright © 2009 by Shaneen Clarke

ISBN: 0-9793192-9-3
978-0-9793192-9-7

Published by

LIFEBRIDGE
BOOKS
P.O. Box 49428
Charlotte, NC 28277

Printed in the United States of America.

DEDICATION

This book is dedicated to Dennis Beedie, an Assemblies of God pastor in Great Britain, who in the 1970s was an usher at Kathryn Khulman's meetings in America. As a child he was unable to speak, but on a Scottish beach he prayed to the Lord for healing in return for silently promising to dedicate his own life to His service. Miraculously healed by the Almighty, pastor Dennis, selfless and humble, influenced and supported the call of God on my life, introducing me to the ministry and writings of some of the greats of the 20th century including R.A. Torrey, A.W. Tozer, Kathryn Kuhlman, Charles Finney, the Jeffreys Brothers and the hymns of Charles Wesley.

I would also like to share my deep appreciation and love to my husband Martin and my two children, Faith and Christopher, for supporting and helping me during the hours of preparation for this book.

Most important, I must bow to and thank My Lord and Savior Jesus Christ for everything He has done for me and for whom I love more than words can express.

He made him ride in the heights
of the earth that he might eat the produce
of the fields; He made him draw honey from
the rock and from the flinty rock.
−DEUTERONOMY 32:13

CONTENTS

INTRODUCTION   7

1   DARE TO FACE ADVERSITY   9

2   DARE TO DREAM   15

3   DARE TO DISCOVER YOUR PURPOSE   23

4   DARE TO DECLARE YOUR FAITH   31

5   DARE TO FORM A TEAM   39

6   DARE TO CHALLENGE YOUR GIANTS   49

7   DARE TO TRANSFORM YOUR THINKING   67

8   DARE TO BURY PROCRASTINATION   77

9   DARE TO BE DISCIPLINED   87

10   DARE TO TAKE CHARGE OF YOUR FINANCES   95

11   DARE TO STAY FOCUSED   115

12   DARE TO STEP INTO GREATNESS   127

INTRODUCTION

*M*illions are trapped by an enemy called "average." As a result of being constantly beaten down by negative circumstances and personal failures, they have settled for second best. Sadly, some have totally given up, thinking there is no way out.

As you will read on these pages, I've been there. But at my lowest ebb, I was able to summon the courage of a young man who lived in Old Testament times. His name was David. And I came to the conclusion that if he could defeat a giant with only one small stone and a powerful God, why couldn't I become a conqueror too?

Regardless of where you are on life's mountain, there is a higher peak waiting to be climbed and a greater vision waiting to be fulfilled.

You are about to learn what your future can become when you discover your destiny, declare your faith, and challenge your giants.

I also want to show you how to transform your

thinking, say farewell to procrastination, find the power to be self-disciplined, and stay focused on your objective.

It is my prayer that you will escape from the rut and routine of mediocrity and pursue your God-given purpose. I know what it means to see a dream transformed from a struggle to reality. And now I want to share these proven principles with you.

Right now is your time to take a giant step forward. Dare to be Great!

– Shaneen Clarke

ONE

DARE TO
FACE ADVERSITY

I know you well; you aren't strong,
but you have tried to obey and have not
denied my Name. Therefore I have opened
a door to you that no one can shut.
—REVELATION 3:8 TLB

*B*orn in London of Indian origin, my parents were always very concerned I would become too "westernized" —and perhaps even a rebel.

As is common in our family culture, I was only fourteen years of age when my father had chosen my future spouse. In fact, I was engaged to be married as soon as I finished school.

During my teen years, however, there was a tugging inside leading me in a direction I could not escape. Day after day, my heart was being pulled by a higher power. I heard God Himself speaking to me, saying, "I have a work for you to do."

A FASCINATING BOOK

As a young girl whose future seemed carefully mapped out for her, I wrestled with who I was and what I was supposed to do in life.

Growing up in a Christian church, I can still remember the day my Scottish pastor handed me a book titled Daughter of Destiny. It was the account of the American woman evangelist, Kathryn Kuhlman. I was fascinated by her story. Here was a woman who went through a divorce and never married again, yet God raised her up to be one of the leading evangelists of her day. Thousands flocked to hear her preach —people would queue up from five o'clock in the morning just to get into the auditorium. And the testimonies of the amazing miracles of healing occurring in her services were beyond anything I had ever heard before.

My pastor was once an usher at Miss Kuhlman's meetings and he shared with me how "When she came on stage, the atmosphere was electric. The presence of God was tangible."

This book became an instrument God placed in my hands to motivate my desire to be used by the person of the Holy Spirit.

From that moment forward I prayed to have such a heaven-sent anointing in my own life.

A Special Relationship

Hungry to understand more, I eagerly studied the lives of great men and women of faith. I began reading books on prayer by A. W. Tozer and the miracles wrought through the inspired ministry of Smith Wigglesworth. They opened my spiritual eyes and gave me insight into having a unique relationship with the Lord.

Determined to know God on an intimate, one on one, level, I was setting my alarm for 4:00 A.M. to pray for two hours before my first classes at college. Then from 6:00 to 8:00 in the evening I found myself reenergized as I read the Word and fellowshipped with Him.

This urgency to grow in faith became my way of life.

During these times I would often experience the presence of the Holy Spirit so powerfully I literally felt a tingling sensation of heat running through my hands. I was learning the keys to entering into a place of communion with God's Spirit.

THE NEWS SPREAD

My heart for the lost began to grow, so much so that my parents allowed me to invite teenagers to our home for a weekly prayer meeting. During these gatherings many found Christ as their personal Savior and the awesome power of God began to fill young lives with the Holy Spirit.

The news spread in our church, and adults were asking to attend the home meetings too.

My passion to serve the Lord also lead me to work in the community with the homeless and those suffering with multiple sclerosis.

Watching my spiritual transformation, one day my pastor asked me to preach in an evening service. As a sixteen-year-old, I was thrilled at this wonderful opportunity the Lord was giving me.

I titled my message what you are now reading: Dare to be Great. It was the biblical account of David and Goliath.

Although I had never personally heard Kathryn Kuhlman preach, there was a picture of her on the front cover of her book wearing an unusual white, flowing dress. My mother, knowing how much I admired this woman of God, arrived home one day having purchased a very similar dress. It was brown and way out of style, but it looked exactly like the one Kathryn was wearing.

I loved high fashion, and this dress was definitely not the look for me, but I dared to wear it when I stood in the pulpit of our church to proclaim God's Word for the first time.

AT A CROSSROADS

Those early years of preparation and zeal continued, and deep inside I longed to enroll in a Bible College. But my father's wishes took preference and I was married at the age of seventeen.

———— ❧ ————

My heart's desire now seemed just a dream—and I tried to accept the reality of my life.

As a married woman, I continued to serve the local church and even preach from time to time, but there were obstacles and challenges that were taking a toll on me.

Before long I reached a critical crossroads. The strain of marrying at such a young age and the pressures within and from our cultural backgrounds were at odds with our European environment.

Particularly the attitude of my husband toward me (such as being denied access to even seeing my parents without prior approval of my mother-in-law). Such customs broke my heart and brought resentment.

Sadly, our marriage disintegrated.

Here I was, a young divorced woman—and I felt like a fugitive, an outcast. I hid myself in my real estate work and my part-time job at a radio station.

Hurting deeply, I tried everything to ease the pain and fill my time by dining in fine restaurants and meeting new people, but there was an emptiness, a void. Something was missing.

Even though I was crushed emotionally, inwardly, the small flame God had ignited in me as a teenager refused to die. The Lord was faithful to His Word; He never left me. Thank God the day dawned when I began dreaming again.

Maybe, just maybe, I could return to what I was called to this earth to become.

TWO

DARE TO DREAM

For the vision is yet for an
appointed time...Though it tarries, wait
for it; because it will surely come.
−HABAKKUK 2:3

*B*efore Leonardo da Vinci painted The Last
Supper, he saw the masterpiece in his mind. Before
Winston Churchill led Britain during World War II,
he envisioned winning the battle. Before Tiger Woods
won his first championship, he saw himself holding
the coveted trophy.

There are times when God gives you a dream so
distinctly that it changes the direction of your life.
This is what He did for Joseph, the son of Jacob, who
saw his rise to leadership and his brothers bowing
before him (Genesis 37:1-11; 42:6).

On other occasions the Lord plants an idea the size
of a tiny mustard seed into your mind and it begins to
germinate and grow.

Think about your own journey. When your obituary is written, what do you want the world to remember about you? Will you leave a permanent, positive mark on those around you? Will you be a person from whom many receive inspiration?

VISUALIZE VICTORY

In my seminars, I often ask people to take out a pen and paper and jot down what they wish to be known for; what they feel the Lord wants them to accomplish. Take a moment and do the same

———— ❦ ————

When you desire to achieve an objective, visualize what you want to become a reality and paint the picture in your mind, including all the details.

You may want to summarize it in the form of a note and place it in your Bible, your car, or on a mirror at home.

You will never savor the thrill of success until you *see* yourself as victorious. However, the opposite is also true. You are never conquered until you accept the image of losing in your mind. As the old adage states: "Be careful what you wish for, because you may get it." What will your choice be? Triumphantly saying "Yes" to victory, or timidly admitting "No" and reaping defeat? I'd rather live by the words of Paul, who said, *"We are more than conquerors through Him who loved us"* (Romans 8:37).

TAKE THREE DEEP BREATHS

Right this minute, place yourself in the driver's seat and picture yourself taking command over and solving a particular problem. This is part of the process of moving into a realm of confidence where other issues will be met and mastered as they arise.

Here is a simple exercise, but well worth trying. Take three long, deep breaths and exhale slowly after each one:

- As you take the first, say to yourself, "I am breathing in confidence; I am breathing out fear."
- With the second: "I am breathing in power; I am breathing out weakness."
- With the third: "I am breathing in victory over my problem (name it); I am breathing out defeat."

17

vision brand new confidence and determination flowing into your being. With God's help you can take control and command of your life.

THE PRODUCER AND THE ACTRESS

Noted author Norman Vincent Peale, in his book, *Positive Imaging*, relates a poignant story of what can happen when imaging is misused.

A psychiatrist friend told Peale of a Hollywood producer who came to him because things were not going well in his professional life.

———— ❧ ————

The man had lost his grip and his career had fallen apart. He couldn't sleep and was in the depths of depression.

Finally the real story emerged. The producer had met an attractive young actress who was trying to get a foothold in her film career. It was the age-old story. Although he was married, he was smitten, and determined to have an affair with this starlet. The girl had scruples and resisted, but the producer was a persuasive and determined man, willing to use the leverage of his position. He was also aware of the power of imaging, and used it to visualize the entire course of seduction: the build-up, timing, and setting. He planned it just like one of his movie scenarios, and the outcome was just as he imaged it to be.

But, unexpectedly, the girl came to the movie mogul and told him she was pregnant. She thought he loved her enough to get a divorce and marry her. Instead, he advised the young woman to have an abortion. In despair, the actress went back to her apartment and took a fatal dose of sleeping pills, leaving a note that implicated the producer.

Even in jaded Hollywood, it was a scandal and the man's career was ruined.

The lesson in this story is that whatever we visualize must always be held up to the light of integrity before we begin traveling down any path.

This is why we must make the Lord our partner in our thoughts. He is the touchstone that will keep our mind and desires on the high moral plane where they belong.

THE BIRTH OF A VISION

Let me share how a dream became a reality in my own life.

Starting several years ago, I became very burdened for business people and ministry in the marketplace.

The seed began as a comment from a Christian acquaintance. I was working out at a health club and

19

a friend asked, "What are you up to these days?"

I responded in the best way I could, wanting to make myself look good. "I've been giving a little help to homeless people," I replied.

Although this was true, it was not a ministry in which I was totally involved.

Then she commented, "Shaneen, business people are not being reached, and those who are successful and wealthy also need the Gospel."

My friend continued, "So many are helping the poor, but what about the marketplace?

It was as if a light bulb had been turned on inside my brain! My mind began to whirl and God began to drop His vision into my spirit.

———❧———

I could see successful women coming together in an elegant atmosphere, receiving and responding to the message of Christ.

TEA AT THE RITZ

With this mustard seed of faith I launched "Tea at the Ritz" in a private dining room at the Ritz Hotel in Piccadilly. If you ever visit London be sure to enjoy the delightful experience of an afternoon tea in this Palm Court setting. Taking tea is quintessentially

English and part of our British heritage.

The women had the excuse of dressing up, feeling special, and relaxing in the height of luxury. Appropriate attire is expected—no jeans or shorts are permitted. Since it opened in 1906, the Ritz has been steeped in the history of the rich and famous.

At one of our events there, on a Valentine's Day, I spoke on the subject of *The 21st Century Woman*. At the close of the meeting I extended an invitation to those who wanted to give their hearts to Jesus. The Spirit of the Lord was present in such a powerful way that one woman literally dropped to the floor under God's anointing.

You can imagine the panic of the butlers and waitstaff. One of them immediately called for an ambulance. This uproar caused the servers to inquire further on what they had witnessed that day. I pray these men will come to the Lord as a result and we will all enjoy High Tea in the courts of heaven!

ADD ACTION TO YOUR DREAM

The Ritz Teas continue and are attended by many unbelievers who leave the portals of this great establishment as changed individuals. God is using the quality of this environment to display His excellence.

Those who know the English understand that they will always take tea at a moment of distress, and there can be no greater crisis than not knowing the Gospel.

By listening, and following God's call, I boldly stepped into a place of excellence to promote the message that offers eternal life.

Amazing opportunities will result when you dare to dream—and put action to your vision.

THREE

DARE TO DISCOVER YOUR PURPOSE

May He grant you according to your heart's desire, and fulfill all your purpose.

−PSALM 20:4

The first step to discovering your true reason for being is to recognize the source of your existence. The Bible teaches, *"For of Him and through Him and to Him are all things, to whom be glory forever"* (Romans 11:36).

To understand our purpose is vital. But some ask, "What does God have to do with this?"

We need to understand that purpose originated with the Creator. As we read, *"In the beginning God created the heaven and the earth. And the earth was without form, and void; and darkness was upon the face of the deep. And the Spirit of God moved upon the face of the waters"* (Genesis 1:1-2 KJV). In other words, God purposed life out of nothing.

The Hebrew word *bara* means to create something completely new. It is used only three times in Scripture—to form matter, life, and man. This tells us there is a uniqueness about our very existence.

The reason the Bible remains the best selling publication in the 21st century is because it is the only book that can totally transform people's lives. Its principles have been tried, tested, and proven to work. Even more, Scripture clearly defines the purpose of mankind.

Today, millions are searching for ways to attain success in business, achieve better relationships, and make a lasting impact.

The answers are not found in the writings, sayings, or philosophies of man, but in the inspired Word of God.

WHAT DO YOU BELIEVE?

A recent widely-read book, *The God Delusion*, was written by British biologist Richard Dawkins, a person who does not believe in the power of God as a Creator, but states he is still "working it out."

Attacks by unbelievers are nothing new. Christianity has been under assault for two thousand years, yet it has survived and is still growing. In fact, many of the most learned men in history have come to the reality of Scripture:

- Professor James Simpson, the 19th century Scottish obstetrician who discovered chloroform (which led to the modern anaesthetic) was once asked, "What is the most important discovery you ever made?" He replied, "The day I discovered Jesus Christ."

- Sir Isaac Newton (1642-1727) perhaps the greatest scientist of all time, wrote religious as well as scientific books and regarded his theological writings as more significant. He felt that no sciences were better tested than the religion of the Bible.

- Michael Faraday (1791-1867), one of the most brilliant scientists of the 19th century, stated the Christian faith was the single most important influence upon him.

- In our generation, actor/director Mel Gibson was so personally impacted by the life of Christ that he produced the widely-heralded film, *The Passion*.

Certainly, there will always be questions raised —just as an eight-year-old innocently asks, "Who made God?"

Despite the attempts by Dawkins and others to postulate their unproven theories, according to the Word, God was not created. Rather He is self-existent. As He told Moses, *"I AM WHO I AM"* (Exodus 3:14).

The concept of a transcendent, eternal God who has always been is certainly difficult to wrap one's mind around. But it is equally difficult to fathom what atheists believe, that everything we see has come out of absolutely nothing!

So what do you believe? That God created something out of nothing? Or that *nothing* created something out of nothing?

A Special Creation

The word "soul" in Genesis 2 has misled many people into thinking that the only factor which makes human beings unique is that we have souls. But there is so much more. We were created in the "image of God" which also affects our spirit—plus we have the ability to make moral judgments.

To believe that man and anthropoid apes come

from common stock is in direct opposition to the biblical account. Without doubt, man is a special creation, formed by Almighty God for an intimate relationship with Him. Out of this is birthed our passion and purpose.

GREAT EXPLOITS

As a young girl, I came to believe in Jesus based on faith—and now the evidence I have experienced has taught me there is much more to life than I could have ever imagined. It has given me purpose and a compelling desire to touch the world around me.

I began to comprehend the heart of God; that He desires for us to know Him deeply and understand His will for our lives. Scripture tells us, *"The people who know their God shall be strong, and carry out great exploits"* (Daniel 11: 32).

———— ❧ ————

Knowing your Creator makes the difference regarding how you see others around you and how you view the gift of life.

"WHY AM I HERE?"

Millions are searching for "a word"—anything that may change their circumstances or tell them about the

SHANEEN CLARKE

future. This is why astrology, horoscopes and fortune tellers are still popular. The *true* Word, however, is found in the pages of Scripture and will help you recover what you may have lost while searching in the wrong places for direction.

———— ❧ ————

We all need a reason to get up in the morning—to have a passion that motivates us to celebrate the day, regardless of our situation.

Still, it is only natural to ask, "Why am I here? What is my reason for being?"

The answer is simple. We have been placed on this earth to fulfill God's will and enjoy what He calls us to pursue.

MORE THAN EMOTIONS

When fervor and purpose dominate our lives, we are spurred to attempt objectives beyond our normal capabilities. You see, the human heart is created for passion, and God desires for us to arise each day with enthusiasm to accomplish His will here on earth.

What a difference to wake up every morning and pray, "Lord, what can You do through me today?"

28

rather than ask, "Lord, will you do this *for* me today?"

Often people relate passion to sex, or just a "feel good" emotion. But it runs much deeper. Passion is a power that helps you recognize there is more to life than simply a positive spirit. To turn it around, what happens when they are *not* feeling good? Does passion depart?

There are three Greek words for Love:

- *Eros*—a sensual, sexual attraction.
- *Phileo*—a friendly love of give and take. When you add *adelphos* (brother) you have Philadelphia, the city of brotherly love.
- *Agape*–a divine self-sacrificial love.

Eros is not a bad word, it simply signifies a response of the flesh, and an emotional, dependent love. However, when it ends, the relationship struggles. Because human nature relies on feelings, many search for something that can resurrect the feeling. It is the reason there are so many divorces.

True passion results from personally experiencing the *agape* love which can only come from God Himself. As a result, the Lord gives you the fuel—or power—to overcome adversity and weakness.

Purpose and passion are intertwined. When you discover your reason for being, you will suddenly have the motivation, enthusiasm, and drive to see it fulfilled.

If your life's calling has never been revealed, don't search for the answers in the local library or a self-help seminar. Get in touch with the source of all greatness. Dare to call on God.

FOUR

DARE TO DECLARE YOUR FAITH

For we walk by faith, not by sight.
– 2 CORINTHIANS 5:7

*W*hen Queen Victoria ascended to the throne of Great Britain in 1837, the nation had created the largest Empire the world had ever seen. The Queen was asked, "What made the Empire great?"

She replied with these two words: "The Bible."

During its rise as a global force, Christianity influenced the very center of power in Britain. As the nation obeyed God's laws, the promise of the Bible came true: *"The Lord will make you the head and not the tail; you shall be above only, and not be beneath, if you heed the commandments of the Lord your God, which I command you today, and are careful to observe them"* (Deuteronomy 28:13).

The Lord had been faithful to His Word.

For generations, Britain achieved more for the cause of Christ than any other nation. For example, William Carey, "The father of modern missions" started a global evangelization movement that would change the world. Dynamic revivalists including John and Charles Wesley and George Whitefield saw mighty moves of God in England and abroad. Men such as William Wilberforce were inspired by their Christian faith to spur the movement to abolish slavery.

As Britain obeyed God's rules, the nation prospered.

———— ❦ ————

History reveals what happens when a society neglects the Almighty because of selfish pride.

The British Empire fell apart and the country saw its power erode.

REVIVAL ON CAMPUS

Through the centuries there have been men and women who have dared to declare their faith. A man named Timothy Dwight was one such individual. Dwight, who was the grandson of Jonathan Edwards, became the president of Yale in 1795. His first baccalaureate message included an invitation for all students to have an open forum on the Christian faith.

At first there was hostility, so Dwight continued preaching truth with love to such an extent that before the school year had finished, more than half the students at Yale professed their faith in Christ.

Think of what happened at Williams College in Massachusetts in the early 1800s. A group of five students met regularly under the branches of a large maple tree. There, they would read the Word, confess their sins, ask for forgiveness and pray that a revival would visit their campus. One night, a violent storm erupted and they ran to an old barn and continued praying around a haystack. Their prayers were answered as a powerful move of God swept the campus. Many church historians trace the start of the Great Awakening to this moment.

It is sad to see how Williams College has become just one more liberal educational institution that has lost the connection of who they were created by and called to have a relationship with.

A "PREACHING HOUSE"

George Whitefield, was a 23-year-old preacher who was touched by the Awakening when it hit England. He sailed across the Atlantic and proclaimed the message of Christ in the Colonies. It is said that his voice was so strong he could be heard by as many as 30,000 in an open field.

Benjamin Franklin was so taken with Whitefield that he built the evangelist a "Preaching house" in Philadelphia—which became the first building of the University of Pennsylvania.

Amherst College is another prime example. It was founded with the objective of training young men to serve God. The school's motto is the Latin phrase, "Terras Irradent"—alluding to Isaiah 6:3: *The whole earth is full of His glory.*

According to author Jay Rogers, "In the early years of the school, powerful revivals were frequent."

Graduates of Amherst College include the social reformer Henry Ward Beecher (brother of Harriet Beecher Stowe), and Daniel W. Poor, the pioneer missionary to Ceylon.

UNDER ATTACK

Today we are so pressured by political correctness that some believers are afraid to even wear the symbol of the cross. I'm not one of those.

I'll never forget shopping in one of the most famous department stores in London when a clerk commented, "I love your cross."

"Thank you," I replied.

Then she continued, "I have just been asked to remove mine."

"Why?" I wanted to know.

"My boss said we are not allowed to wear any religious symbol." How sad.

———❧———

In a nation where the Church of England is the officially established Christian church, Christ is under attack.

Schools are pressured regarding how and when they can mention the name of Jesus. It's as if the precious cross of Calvary has been covered with a veil.

IT STARTS AT HOME

Oh, how far we have drifted.

In the introduction to his book, *The Bible Lessons of John Quincy Adams for His Son,* author Doug Phillips shares this significant fact:

> *In 1800, President Thomas Jefferson commissioned a national survey conducted by Dupont de Numours to determine the status of literacy in America. The results were phenomenal. Better than ninety-seven percent of American citizens could read and write. The stated reason for this success was that, from Boston to Atlanta, American fathers practiced daily Bible reading with their children around the breakfast table. Long before the creation of government schools (public schools) or the National Education Association, faithful fathers proved that the simple act of teaching the Holy Scriptures to their children at home would lead our nation to become the most literate in the world.*

How I pray that the Word of God will return to the dinner menu in our homes. When this begins to happen, even one household at a time, families will become whole again and the nation will be blessed. The sad fact is that parents and children are not even eating together, so how can they bring God into their relationship?

Jewish families practice the Shabbat on a Friday, which always gives time to the reading of the Torah. The custom is for parents to bless their children with biblical blessings of Ephraim and Manasseh. The parent (traditionally the father but in many homes now both father and mother) places their two hands on the child's head and says to the son: "May God make you a symbol of blessing as He did Ephraim and Manasseh." To the daughter: "May God make you a symbol of blessing as He did to Sarah, Rebekah, Rachel, and Leah."

There is also a blessing for the husband: "He shall command His messengers to guard over you wherever you go." And in some Jewish homes, a husband sings to his wife the words of Proverbs 31 (A woman of valor).

My Jewish friends have told me that often the children grow up and want to bless their younger siblings.

THE BEST YOU CAN BE

I believe *every* family needs to invite God's favor into their home and on their family members. Let these words flow from your heart as often as possible:

"The Lord bless you and keep you; the Lord make His face shine upon you, and be gracious to you; the Lord lift up His countenance upon you, and give you peace" (Numbers 6:24-26).

———————⟨⟩———————

Do everything in your power to tap into the greatness found in the Word of God.

It will not only bless your home, but help you become the best you can be on this earth.

Dare to bring the reading of the Word back to the dinner table. If you desire to have a God-honoring family, this is a wonderful place to share your faith.

FIVE

DARE TO FORM A TEAM

Two are better than one, because they have a
good reward for their labor. For if they fall, one will
lift up his companion. But woe to him who is alone
when he falls, for he has no one to help him.
—ECCLESIASTES 5:9-10

*I*n London, while teaching a monthly series on the subject of prayer, I had the opportunity to read many accounts of how God used individuals and small groups to impact society. I was especially thrilled to learn the story of a man in New York City named Jeremiah Lanphier.

In the 1850s the city was known as a modern day Babylon, certainly not the epicenter for evangelical Christianity. Yet, because of this gentleman, it became the launching point for a revival that is said to have produced over one million converts at a time when the U.S. population was only about thirty million.

Surprisingly, very few today have ever heard of the Layman's Prayer Revival.

A MIRACLE IN MANHATTAN

In 1857, many churches in the United States were experiencing a decline in church attendance. A Dutch Reformed Church on Fulton Street in Manhattan decided they needed to have more outreach into the community. They noticed that between noon and one o'clock most businessmen took their lunch break. (It's a little different today where you can see customers at a fast food restaurant, answering their Blackberry's, taking text messages and sending emails—even while eating. Out of the corner of their eye they are watching cable news on a wide screen).

Well, the Manhattan church actually "hired" a businessman, Jeremiah Lanphier, to offer a noontime hour of prayer. He handed out 20,000 flyers advertising the first prayer meeting to be held September 23, 1857.

Only six men showed up.

After they prayed, Jeremiah told everyone they would meet again next week—same time, same place. The word spread and seven days later twenty men were in attendance. The next week there were forty and those present decided to make these prayer meetings *daily* instead of weekly.

A NATION ON ITS KNEES

After a few months the meetings grew to 3,000 and they had to move to a nearby YMCA. Churches in Manhattan became involved and newspapers started reporting the growing phenomenon. This movement began to spread to other cites. There were now 3,000 in Jayne's Hall in Philadelphia, 2,000 meeting in the Metropolitan Hall of Chicago. Soon, in nearly every city from Maine to California you could find one of these prayer meetings.

Everyone was welcome and people could come and go as they needed, but certain rules were established. There was no denominational emphasis, no controversial statements were allowed, nor announcements of a specific church's events. Only prayer requests that were submitted in writing could be read aloud. And the prayer time ended promptly at one o'clock.

One unbeliever attended and heard a submitted prayer request for an unsaved son, which happened to be from his own mother requesting prayer for him. Many found salvation at these meetings.

41

A customer asked a merchant if he was going to close his business at noon to go and pray, The shop owner replied, "Yes, I must. Why don't you come with me?"

It was quite common to see signs in Manhattan and other cities that read "We will re-open at the close of the prayer meeting."

It is estimated that 50,000 people in New York alone came to Christ and about a million across the U.S. This revival is seen as a reaction to two major societal issues at the time. The first is the Panic of 1857 which occurred the month before the prayer meetings began. This was a major economic crisis where over 5,000 businesses failed in one year. The second major issue was the problem of slavery.

The great tension over this led to the start of the Civil War two years later—the same time as the end of this move of God.

SHAKE OFF THE DOUBT

I believe God is still calling committed men and women to follow their vision and step out in faith. In fact, you may be the one who brings the power and anointing of God's Spirit to your community, and it may spread to the entire world. Times may have changed, but the need to launch out for the Kingdom has not.

―――――♋―――――

*Whether it is a prayer group or other
ministry, the principle of "faith without
works is dead" still stands.*

I pray you will be empowered to work out the faith
and shake off the doubt.

THE "CLAPHAM SECT"

Over the centuries, God has called various groups
at specific times for certain purposes. Let me tell you
about one which was formed to raise the spiritual and
moral tone of a nation.

In the late 1700s there was a small group in London
called the Clapham Sect who banded together for
prayer. Their numbers were small, but they had wide
and important connections and influence and they
shared a common goal of changing society for the
better.

These men and women included directors of the
Sierra Leone Company, the founders of the Church
Missionary Society and members of the Abolitionist
Committee. The group eventually included historians,
lawyers, bankers, writers, and members of Parliament
—notables such as abolitionist William Wilberforce,

banker Henry Thornton and author Hannah More.

CHANGING THE CULTURE

Although they frequently differed on political matters, they were of one mind when it came to social and moral questions. As a result, these evangelical Anglicans became a force to be reckoned with.

———— ❧ ————

Many say there was never such an influential group of Christians in Britain before or since.

Their efforts were rewarded with the passage of the Slave Trade Act in 1807 and the Slavery Abolition Act of 1833, resulting in the total banning of the trade throughout the British Empire and, after many further years of campaigning, the total emancipation of British slaves. They also campaigned vigorously for Britain to wield its influence to eradicate slavery throughout the world.

It is said that after the Bill for Abolition had passed in the Commons by a large majority, Wilberforce turned to Thornton and said, "Well, Henry, What shall we abolish now?

Thornton, thought for a moment and replied, "The Lottery, I think."

Because of the efforts of this group, at the time the Lottery did go—and they didn't stop there. Wilberforce and his friends in Clapham have been credited for the high moral standards of early Victorian England. There had truly been a reformation of manners and morals in the nation.

An Undeniable Work

In 1829, Francis Place, who was not an evangelical, wrote, "I am certain I risk nothing when I assert that more good has been done to the people in the last thirty years than in the three preceding centuries; that during this period they have become wiser, better, more frugal, more honest, more respectable, more virtuous than they ever were before."

The Clapham Sect was chided in their day as "the saints," but their work was undeniable. They published a Journal, The Christian Observer, and were also credited with establishing several missionary and tract societies, including the British and Foreign Bible Society.

What is His Will?

If you truly want to know a person's last will and testament, you must read it. Suppose a wife bemoaned,

"My husband, who was extremely rich, has just passed away. I wish I knew whether he left me anything in his will."

I would respond, "Why don't you read the document. It's all there."

And if we want to understand the Lord's wishes on a subject, we open the pages of the Word and discover His intentions.

————— ❧ —————

It is God's perfect will for you to have a vision, because without it you will perish (Proverbs 29:18).

And, if you read the Scriptures, you'll find it is His will for you to unite with other believers to accomplish His purpose. As the Bible says, *"Let each of you look out not only for his own interests, but also for the interests of others"* (Philippians 2:4). God will bless us as we "serve him shoulder to shoulder" (Zephaniah 3:9 NIV).

MULTIPLY THE MESSAGE

I believe the Lord has something fresh and exciting to pour into your spirit. He wants to reveal His vision for your future. As Scripture declares, *"Behold, the former things have come to pass, and new things I declare; Before they spring forth I tell you of them"* (Isaiah 42:9).

Pray for these words to become a reality. God is patiently waiting to unveil His plan—and for you to unite with other believers to multiple the message.

In this new day He will do a new thing. Reach out and embrace what the Lord is sending your way.

SIX

DARE TO CHALLENGE YOUR GIANTS

*David said to Goliath, "You come to me with a
sword, with a spear, and with a javelin. But I come
to you in the name of the Lord of hosts."*

—1 SAMUEL 17:45

*I*n chapter one I mentioned how I was asked to
preach my first sermon at the age of sixteen. My "Dare
to Be Great" message was centered on the story of
David and Goliath.

Without question, every man, woman, and child
either has or will encounter a scenario of facing a
mammoth problem, where adversity brings either
success or failure.

Many are slain or conquered by a formidable

giant—fearful of the noise he makes or the negative words he uses, such as "You can't do it," or "Who do you think you are?"

The voice grows louder, then he hounds you with bills you can't pay, and entices you with habits that rob you of your destiny, or causes disappointments that hold you back.

Paralyzed with fear, your mind is immersed in despair and self pity. It's as if you are hiding in a box, saying, "I don't care what anybody thinks. I'm not coming out!"

We all face adversity, but how we handle it speaks volumes concerning who we are.

———— ❧ ————

Circumstances can either defeat and destroy you or give you the determination to thrive.

Often when we encounter obstacles, we are in such a state of shock we become immobilized and freeze. In this gridlock mode, we may not know what to do, so we do nothing, then react impulsively without thinking. As a result we make poor decisions.

BEYOND ASSUMPTION

From personal experience I can tell you how wrong choices made under stress can cost time, money, energy, and friends. God's Word tells us, *"If you faint in the day of adversity, your strength is small"* (Proverbs 24:10).

On the field of battle in Israel, there was no one who stepped forward and asked, "Can I go out and face the giant?" But David dared to be great.

When I was a young girl preaching this message, I remember saying what I thought David would have said: "I'm going to knock his head off!"

Today, when difficulties occur, I stop and calmly ask myself, "What can I do about this?" I examine the pros and cons to see a more objective, less emotional picture of the situation. Most of us need time and space to think clearly.

David did not assume he would defeat Goliath, he knew it! The word *assumption* is a noun, a feeling we have that something must be true, but we have no proof.

The difference between assumption and faith is

that the first is a feeling, the second is based on fact. The Bible tells us, *"Now faith is the substance of things hoped for, the evidence of things not seen"* (Hebrews 11:1). When you operate in faith, thank God, there is no more doubt.

THE SOURCE OF ASSURANCE

David's faith had enabled him to place his confidence in the Lord without reservation. His belief was kindled by his intimacy with God—knowing His characteristics of justice, mercy, and power. It was this inner strength that caused him to act with total assurance and authority.

This same belief can work wonders today. Through it we can command or change circumstances.

———❧———

Faith will always move you to physical or mental action.

It carries confidence of the fulfilment of things hoped for. It is alive—a living substance. I dare you to draw on the measure of faith you have and release it now.

JEALOUS BROTHERS

As David neared the field of battle he could see that all Israel was filled with anxiety because of the challenge of this Philistine named Goliath. But young David was fired up and ready to preserve the honor of the living God and reputation of His people. The armies of Israel were downtrodden and their courage failed them.

David's brothers were standing on the edge of the battlefield when he arrived, and they immediately became suspicious, even jealous. Remember, they had been at home when Samuel came in search of a future king. His silent departure had awakened in their minds the real object of Samuel's visit. Now their envy had been aroused as they saw David being honored above them, and they did not regard him with respect and brotherly love.

LIONS AND BEARS

David had ultimate confidence that he could defeat Goliath. When Saul questioned his ability to fight, David answered:

53

"'Your servant used to keep his father's sheep, and when a lion or a bear came and took a lamb out of the flock, I went out after it and struck it, and delivered the lamb from its mouth; and when it arose against me, I caught it by its beard, and struck and killed it. Your servant has killed both lion and bear; and this uncircumcised Philistine will be like one of them, seeing he has defied the armies of the living God.' Moreover David said, 'The Lord, who delivered me from the paw of the lion and from the paw of the bear, He will deliver me from the hand of this Philistine'" (1 Samuel 17:34-37).

This challenge Goliath made to Israel has a deep spiritual significance. The loser of this confrontation would become the winner's slave. Israel turning into the Philistine's servants typifies a soul being enslaved to doubt, fear, hopelessness, or all negative spiritual attributes. In fact the meaning of the Hebrew words Goliath and Philistine convey this. In this context, Goliath denotes "revealing or conspicuous." Philistine is derived from the root Hebrew word which means "to deviate from the truth" or "to roll or wallow in dust."

THE BACKSTAGE OF LIFE

What David did as a shepherd boy protecting his flock, killing bears and lions, taught him to work with what he had, whether it was his bare hands or a sling. It prepared him for the giant bellowing, "I dare you!"

There comes a moment in each of our lives when we are challenged to do what no one else has the courage to try. What we have done previously is the key to releasing us for the present. It is what we have silently worked and prayed for:

- Where no one could praise you
- Where no one noticed who you are
- Where your motives were pure and innocent

This is what really prepares you for that special encounter. It does not just happen because you say so. Jesus, the Son of the living God, had to undergo the isolation of the wilderness, the voice of Satan, emotional pain, and nights of temptation. Only after all this was He ready to bring the message of His

Father to the world. The wilderness encounter was
preparing Jesus for the great moments of His ministry.

———❧———

*What you are prepared to do in your
private life will determine the outcome
of what you dare to accomplish.*

FACING THE ISSUE HEAD-ON

I believe we must always be married to Kingdom
principles, even though the methods may change. As
King Solomon wrote, *"The integrity of the upright will
guide them, but the perversity of the unfaithful will
destroy them"* (Proverbs 11:3).

On the battlefield, Goliath brought out the lack of
faith of the Israelites in God, who had fought and won
all their battles for them. Adversity manifested the
earthly principles of fear, doubt, and weakness (which
are the works of the flesh. Galatians 5:19-20.)

The warriors of Israel couldn't conceive in their
hearts and minds an image of overcoming the giant
because they were crippled by their fear and the
outward appearance of Goliath.

———— ❧ ————

We need to address every situation head-on like David. He saw an open door of opportunity to confront his giant and seized it.

Many stare at doors not even aware if they are open, let alone realizing their significance.

A NEGATIVE HOLD

Years ago I heard this saying and have never forgotten the words: "What you confront will die. What you tolerate will dominate."

We all have stories of sleepless nights, financial problems, even personality traits that get us into trouble. I've heard people complain, "My boss doesn't like me," or "My wife never stops nagging." The list goes on and on and people everywhere struggle with similar issues.

In looking back on those I have counseled, there is a common denominator. You always find a negative aspect of life that is holding the person back from stepping into their destiny.

START REACHING

Earlier we mentioned how many are trapped in the box within. But how do you escape? Or perhaps I should ask: do you even want to come out?

Deciding to break free will challenge your thinking. It will require a decision that no one else can make for you. In fact, it is your chance to take the gift of life seriously.

You only walk on this earth once, so why live constrained in a box that prevents you from realizing your dreams. Everything starts with a choice, yet some decisions are extremely difficult to make because we allow self-imposed limitations to hinder us. Your change begins by opening up to new experiences:

- Closely observe people who are different from how you live and think
- Read new subjects
- Develop a love for learning
- Explore new cultures, places, and traditions
- Attempt something you have never done before

Let me encourage you to make a list of things you have always desired to accomplish or experience. As the apostle Paul writes, *"I do not count myself to have apprehended; but one thing I do, forgetting those things which are behind and reaching forward to those things which are ahead"* (Philippians 3:13).

Here we find the key to escaping from the box of the past. It begins by "reaching out."

The word *reaching* is defined as to "arrive at," "get to," or "extend" toward a particular objective. When we say "the leaders reached an agreement," we are indicating they put together, negotiated, or hammered out what they could agree upon.

Those who dare to be great have to "hammer out" the past. In this case it needs to be smashed into oblivion and totally forgotten!

Personally, after the pain and heartache caused by divorce, I could have retreated into my shell and become bitter for life. However, God had other plans.

As I stood on the promises of the Word and began to pursue the vision He had placed within me, the Lord, in His own surprising way, sent the person who would become my husband and loving partner in life —Martin Clarke, who also embraced God's will for his future.

NECESSARY INGREDIENTS

Every person has a problem-solving potential inside them. But when that potential is blocked by a defeatist, pessimistic attitude, the situation may seem difficult or overwhelming to solve.

Yes, problems are painful at the time, yet they are necessary ingredients for success and are actually beneficial for you. In reality, all worthwhile achievements are the result of dealing with adversities. For example, if you don't exercise your body you will get flabby physically. Likewise, those who never face difficulties become "soft" both mentally and spiritually.

In the midst of it all you may be crying out, "Why does God allow this to happen?" The answer is because He knows you will be strengthened in the process.

MY WORST NIGHTMARE

At one point in my life I found myself at the center of a severe monetary crisis. My husband, Martin, was challenged by a man who sought to seize his business—and his claims included every corner of his estate, including the home we owned.

We faced a formidable foe with deep pockets.

I can still remember the day I was looking out the window of a building in one of London's most prestigious locations at the center of the financial world. It was there I raised my eyes toward heaven and said, "Lord, I surrender. Take whatever I have and use me. If this is what is required to become Your anointed servant, I give it all to You."

At this point, nothing else mattered.

———— ❧ ————

I remembered how Abraham took his son, Isaac, and placed him on the altar. I, too, saw everything I possessed being sacrificed.

I didn't know how to break the news to my children. It was my worst nightmare, but deep inside there was a calming peace because through surrender my purpose became even more alive.

During that tumultuous year, the call of God on my life was raised to the next level. By seeing all my ego-driven emotions die, I was left with the will to yield my all to the Lord.

The situation was brought into court and our attorney said, "In my thirty-five years of practice I have never seen such a vicious attempt of one person to destroy another."

We fought and stood on God's Word according to the promise that no wisdom, no insight, or no plan can succeed against the Lord (Proverbs 21:30). The Bible also says, *"The horse is prepared for the day of battle, but deliverance is of the Lord"* (Proverbs 21:31).

A "RED SEA" EXPERIENCE

During this struggle I was contending with what I considered an evil spirit operating through human personalities. I claimed this verse: *"The wicked man does deceptive work, but he who sows righteousness will have a sure reward"* (Proverbs 11:18).

It reminded me of the children of Israel being chased by the Egyptian armies into the Red Sea. Pharaoh thought he would finally have his revenge. But his wicked plan backfired as his armies were drowned.

———— ❧ ————

The God of the impossible can turn up at any time—even the last minute.

Have you been there? The Almighty allows us to have a "Red Sea" experience in order to display His glory.

The date had arrived for the final decision at the High Court in London.

About one week prior, I had a dream of a great hall with amazing chandeliers and a very shiny, highly polished black and white floor. Suddenly, a monkey-like human with twisted limbs leapt before me. On seeing this in my dream, I pleaded the blood of Jesus—and the figure immediately disappeared!

As I entered the High Court that day, I saw the same chandeliers and the black and white marble of the floors. But now I had an inner peace and thought of the words: *"In all these things we are more than conquerors through Him who loved us"* (Romans 8:37).

I glanced around the room and the atmosphere was tense with anticipation.

As I sat down, to my right was a woman with her eyes closed and her hands were projected out toward the judge. I wasn't sure what this meant, but throughout the hearing I was praying in the name of Jesus.

The arguments swayed back and forth as the battle was in full fury.

It resembled the war we fight with Satan every day. The Bible warns, he comes to *"steal, and to kill, and to destroy"* (John 10:10). But if you keep reading you learn that victory is ours.

When the judge issued his final ruling, I was praising God. We won the case!

YOUR GOLIATH MOMENT

There is a time when you must dare to take a challenge no one else will accept—when it looks as if all odds are against you. Read the biographies of William Wilberforce, Corrie ten Boom, and Martin Luther King and you will understand what it means to stand for faith, justice, and truth.

Today, we have the opportunity to take a stand against abortion, human cloning, drugs, pornography and other moral issues.

A personal declaration brings you from your past into the future of your destiny, and it will cause you to do more than you ever expected. New opportunities suddenly begin to appear.

CHANGED LIVES

Once when I was working in employment recruitment, I talked with disabled people and found that many were not getting jobs—even though a certain percentage in this category had to be employed by corporations. So I decided to be a voice for these individuals and arranged interviews for them.

I was forceful and tireless in telling companies that failing to hire the handicapped was discrimination. It resulted in many lives being changed, including mine!

Even though there may be giants looming on the horizon, remember, a loving God can give you exactly what is needed—not only to challenge them, but to rejoice in victory!

SEVEN

DARE TO TRANSFORM YOUR THINKING

*Set your mind on things
above, not on things on the earth.*

−COLOSSIANS 3:2

*A*s a young woman there were times when my mind seemed to be a magnet for thoughts of emotional disappointment. I was being reminded of past hurts —feelings that were trapped in yesterday. And these thoughts were setting me up for failure.

It was only when I turned to the Word of God that I found the answers I was searching for. Scripture counseled me, *"And do not be conformed to this world, but be transformed by the renewing of your mind, that you may prove what is that good and acceptable and perfect will of God"* (Romans 12:2).

I realized that I had to take control of my thought life. But how was this possible? Could I do it on my own? Then I read that as a believer all things become new, including our thinking. Here is what causes the transformation: when God's Son becomes our Savior and dwells inside, *"We have the mind of Christ"* (1 Corinthians 2:16).

----------✨----------

Think of it! The very thoughts of an omnipotent, all-knowing God are now within us.

FINDING THE SOLUTION

As I look at the lives of successful people, what separates those who reach the top from those who lag behind is good thinking—the ability to creatively analyze, process, and organize thoughts and ideas.

Author Edward de Bono says, "Sometimes the situation is only a problem because it is looked at in a certain way. Looked at in another way, the right course of action may be so obvious that the problem no longer exists."

I have observed that no matter how articulate a

person is, where they have been educated, or how they look, dress, or present themselves, if they don't possess the ability to think clearly, the world will not pay attention.

AS YOU THINK

Thousands of years ago, long before the days of psychologists and psychiatrists, King Solomon wrote, *"For as he thinketh in his heart, so is he"* (Proverbs 23:7).

This has been proven again and again. In the words of author Lee Warren, "It should come as no surprise to anyone, especially medical science with all its technological innovations, that if our minds and souls are brimming with negative principles, our health, in general, will deteriorate and disease will be rampant in the world today. The streets, alleys, Skid Row, and mental institutions throughout the earth plane are crowded with those slain by the Goliath of hopelessness. Man-made philosophies, dogmas, and religions stultified with ceremonies, rituals, and traditions have been unable to and have languished in dealing with this problem. They have failed to instill in the minds of the masses, a knowledge of the principle of faith in the Creator within them."

FROM THOUGHTS COME ACTIONS

Changing our thought-process requires choices we must make every day. If we think defeat, that's what will result, but if we focus on success we will ultimately triumph.

Inspirational writer William Arthur Ward believes, "Nothing limits achievement like small thinking; Nothing expands possibilities like unleashed thinking."

A radical change in our thought life produces a change in actions—which results in healthier emotions and a better way of living. It's like a chain reaction. What we think determines who we are. Who we are determines what we do. As philosopher John Locke observed, "The actions of man are the best interpreters of their thoughts."

This is biblical since Scripture tells us, *"Keep your heart with all diligence, for out of it spring the issues of life"* (Proverbs 4:23).

CHANGE THE SEED!

To achieve success, we don't need to be taught what to think, but how to think. This is why most education and knowledge-based information fails. It's not only facts we need, rather the ability to process and apply what we have learned.

You can't plant red grapes and expect to harvest white grapes. Even if you water and fertilize them every day you can't change the color. What is the answer? If you don't like the crop you are reaping, change the seed you are sowing!

Start planting seeds of creative, solid, profitable thinking. Remember, *"For God has not given us a spirit of fear, but of power and of love and of a sound mind"* (2 Timothy 1:7).

CHOOSE CAREFULLY

After being devastated by setbacks in my own life, I found that part of renewing my dreams included carefully choosing those with whom I would associate. You can have all the vision in the world, but if you hang around with losers, their negative outlook will drain you of every ounce of optimism.

———— ❧ ————

***Right thinking is multiplied
when it is encouraged by like-minded,
affirmative people.***

71

I also had to learn to change my vocabulary, to speak with expectancy and hope instead of fear and dread. Why? Because what you say can become a self-fulfilling prophecy. It is true that *"You are snared by the words of your mouth"* (Proverbs 6:2).

THE PRAYER FACTOR

The best way to know the mind of Christ is to spend time in His presence. This means we must take a break from our busy schedule to get alone with God.

I have come to the conclusion that it is impossible to change your thought life without divine help, This is why our personal prayer time is not only profitable —it is *essential.*

I wholeheartedly agree with the statement that no man is greater than his prayer life.

SPURGEON'S SECRET

Charles Haddon Spurgeon, the noted British preacher, was converted at the age of sixteen and began preaching three years later. By the time he was twenty-seven the people in London built a tabernacle seating 6,000 that was packed several times each week to hear his sermons.

What was the secret to Spurgeon's success?

Spending time alone with the Lord. He is quoted as saying, "If you should ask me for an epitome of the Christian religion, I should say that it is in one word—Prayer."

It's been said that the secret of praying is praying in secret—where you can't show off your gifts or impress those around you. Only the Lord is listening.

In the words of Jesus, *"When you pray, go into your room, and when you have shut your door, pray to your Father who is in the secret place; and your Father who sees in secret will reward you openly"* (Matthew 6:6).

CLEARING THE PATH

If you want to achieve more and reach an objective faster, settle the matter in prayer before you even begin. It will remove doubt and clear the path to both personal and spiritual success. Prayer helps you to have the mind of God and moves your heart to the place of total surrender where the Holy Spirit is able to position you to accomplish exceptional things for the Kingdom.

———————❧———————

To heighten your prayer time, experience the power of silence.

I know it's difficult to go for a period of time saying nothing, but in this intimate setting you will enjoy the fellowship of the Holy Spirit as never before.

"BE STILL AND KNOW"

I remember going on a "silent retreat" for a week-end, and will never forget how difficult it was to keep my mouth shut! There were people at breakfast who grinned and nodded, and somehow we communicated without words. It was a time of deep introspection and communion with the Lord.

The Almighty says, *"Be still, and know that I am God"* (Psalm 46:10).

The presence of the Spirit will bring you to a place of serenity and rest and will hide you from the swirl and noise of society. In the words of the psalmist, *"He who dwells in the secret place of the Most High shall abide under the shadow of the Almighty"* (Psalm 91:1).

The stillness will not only bring an understanding of the deep things of God, it is also a time when the Lord will download you with ideas, inspiration, and wisdom. This is where divine secrets are revealed and the right motivation is received.

Prayer will help you elevate your thoughts to a new and higher plane. As a result, it will affect your total outlook on life. The apostle Paul said it best when he wrote, *"Finally, brethren, whatsoever things are true, whatsoever things are honest, whatsoever things are just, whatsoever things are pure, whatsoever things are lovely, whatsoever things are of good report; if there be any virtue, and if there be any praise, think on these things"* (Philippians 4:8).

Today, will you dare to transform your thinking?

EIGHT

DARE TO BURY PROCRASTINATION

*The desire of the lazy man kills
him, for his hands refuse to labor.*

– PROVERBS 21:25

S ince you only live once, time is a precious
commodity, and something you can't afford to waste.

The minutes and hours you have been granted are
a gift from God, and how you manage them will
determine whether your dreams will be fulfilled.

A billion times a day, a billion people say, "I don't
have enough time." It's a universal problem.

In the words of an unknown writer:

The clock is my dictator, I shall not rest.
It makes me lie down only when exhausted
It leads me into deep depression.
It hounds my soul

It leads me in circles of frenzy, for activities' sake.
Even though I run frantically from task to task, I
will never get it all done.
For my idea is with me.
Deadlines and my need for approval, they drive me.
They demand performance from me, beyond the
limits of my schedule.
They anoint my head with migraines,
My in-basket overflows.
Surely fatigue and time pressures shall follow me.
All the days of my life.
And I will dwell in the bonds of frustration
Forever.

THE DANGER SIGNS

"Thou shalt not procrastinate," may not be one of the Ten Commandments, but it is certainly implied since the Creator gave us six days to do our work and the seventh to rest. Some people turn that around and spend more time resting than putting their hand to the plow.

There are several signs that let you know if you have a procrastination problem. They may include seeing the same projects remain on your "To Do" list day after day, finding yourself wanting to take a tea or coffee break when you have an urgent deadline to meet. Or perhaps saying "Yes" to unimportant requests of others (which fills your time) instead of tackling the pressing jobs already on your list.

If you are honest with yourself, you know exactly when you are in the delay mode. However, to be sure, you first need to know your priorities.

———— ❧ ————

Putting off an unimportant task isn't always procrastination; it may be good prioritization. Learn to recognize the difference.

Why you postpone things can depend on both you and the job at hand. But we usually avoid what needs to be done because (1) we either find the chore unpleasant or (2) the project seems overwhelming.

DIVIDE AND CONQUER

How do you begin to solve the problem?

Start by writing down the tasks you are facing. If they seem large, break them down into component elements. If they are still too daunting, divide them again. Continue the process until you have listed every "sub-task" that is required.

A good rule of thumb is to create a series of work sessions that will take an hour or two each.

Once you've done this, give each job a priority, 1

for high through 10 for low—or A, B, C, D, etc., on a descending scale.

If you have assigned high priority to numerous things, go over the list again and demote the least important.

Your new priorities will represent a plan that you can use to separate the vital from the trivial.

THE TOP TWENTY

Over the years, and from a variety of sources, I've created a list that will help bury procrastination. Here's my top twenty:

1. Set a personal goal to handle each piece of paper that crosses your path only once—either act on it, file it, or throw it away.

2. Never start a job, only to complete a small portion, then place it back on the "To Do" list. Have a total, workable plan for each project.

3. Begin the day with one task you can finish in a short time. You will enjoy that "productive" feeling.

4. Be creative in finding new ways to accomplish the same jobs.

5. Examine the tendency to say "Yes" without fully taking stock of the request. Ask as many questions as necessary regarding what is involved and understand what is truly expected of you.

6. Identify and make a conscious effort to eliminate anything that is wasting your time and effort.

7. Make good use of a daily activity planner and stick to it.

8. On your daily schedule, carve out moments for preparation and creative thinking.

9. Consider new technologies that may increase your efficiency and shorten your workload. Ask yourself honestly, "Will this save me time or just create more headaches?"

10. Make a concerted effort to manage your emails and phone calls. If not, they'll wind up managing you!

11. Check your messages at planned, specific times, rather than jumping whenever there is an incoming email.

12. Watch out for unexpected phone calls and reduce your availability to take them.

13. Don't make the mistake of starting several projects at once, even if you call yourself a "multi-task" person. It's not the most efficient way to deal with your work.

14. Learn to delegate and let others know you have confidence in them. If the results aren't as you would do them, still thank them and move on.

15. Don't always make decisions on the spot. Ask for time to give the request prayerful consideration.

16. Spending too much effort in planning is just one more form of procrastination.

17. Set a "finish date" for the completion of each task.

18. Be careful of the "perfection trap." Trying to make each project absolutely flawless, is another excuse for delay. Instead, focus on progress.

19. Make the job fun. Play some new music, take a break, reward yourself when the job is completed.

20. At the end of each day, review your progress and write your action plan for tomorrow.

START NOW

Analyze where your minutes and hours go. Keep a chart for a couple of weeks so you will have a visual record of how you are spending (or wasting) your valuable time. As a result of what you learn, start rescheduling some of your activities.

Now and again I place myself on a "phone fast" so I can concentrate on what I really need to be doing. Incoming calls, if not well managed, will become a thief of your time and energy.

Since procrastination is a habit that has taken years to take root, don't expect overnight change.

It's been said that our lives are not like rockets that can veer ninety degrees in a few seconds. They are more like cruise ships that must either turn slowly or risk structural damage.

Your most important move is to simply begin.

MAKE THE HOURS COUNT

As believers, we have an obligation to be *"redeeming the time"* (Ephesians 5:16) because *"the night is coming when no one can work"* (John 9:4).

Charles Hummel, an InterVarsity leader, made this observation:

Jesus regularly took time alone with His Father for guidance as well as fellowship in prayer. Mark records an extremely busy day. It began with teaching and healing in the synagogue, and ended well after sunset, when the people "brought to [Jesus] all who were sick and those who were demon-possessed...He healed many who were sick with various diseases" (Mark 1:32, 34).

Nevertheless, very early the next morning, Jesus went off to a solitary place to pray. As a result, he made the incredibly difficult decision to leave the urgent needs of the suffering people already gathering back at the house. "Let us go into the next towns, that I may preach there also, because for this purpose I have come forth." He said (verse 38). His Father's purpose, and not urgent need, shaped his service.

Jesus becomes our Lord and Savior, then provides our example for living (1 Peter 2:21). He has also promised us the Holy Spirit to guide and empower our ministry. In this light, we see that our problem is not managing our time, but ourselves. More accurately, our lives need to be managed by the Lord whom we love and serve. So our basic question is simply this: How can we make our hours and days count for the work God has given us to complete?

――――――❧――――――

I have found that when my tasks are related to my vision or mission, I am more enthusiastic about tackling them.

Any kind of delay is costly, but don't put off making your spiritual decisions, or it may be too late. *"For you yourselves know perfectly that the day of the Lord so comes as a thief in the night. For when they say, 'Peace and safety' then sudden destruction comes upon them...and they shall not escape"* (1 Thessalonians 5:2-3).

Nike® has an advertising slogan that you should adopt for every endeavor you undertake—"Just Do It!"

NINE

DARE TO BE DISCIPLINED

Apply your heart to discipline
and your ears to words of knowledge.
−PROVERBS 23:12 NASB

$\mathcal{L}$ ike so many others, I wrestled with the issue of self-discipline, getting into a pattern of only doing things when I felt like it. Living in London near all the choice boutiques, I would often toddle off to the trendy stores or just hang out in the coffee shops where I would let my feelings lead me astray from my dreams.

During the day, my cell phone would ring, text messages and emails would arrive, and when the sun went down I would sometimes ask myself, "Shaneen, what did you do toward your goal today?"

Sadly, I was ashamed of my answer because I had been waylaid by the lack of discipline.

The day finally came when I knew I could no longer continue this behavior because it was robbing me of my God-given destiny. What was living inside of me, my dream, had to be birthed.

I was the only one who could decide which was more important, letting the hours leisurely drift by, or actively pursuing the vision the Lord had placed within my heart.

DREAM-STEALERS

Take a long, hard look at your own schedule. How much time each day do you spend working toward your ultimate goal? What is getting in the way?

Perhaps a better question would be, "Am I really committed toward my objective?"

Research has shown that during office hours at work, the average person spends nearly forty percent of his or her time in idle conversation and socializing.

As statistics imply, there is plenty of room for improvement.

Self-control includes setting aside specific hours every day that you will devote 100 percent toward moving yourself closer to your target. Even fifteen or thirty minutes, if totally focused, will make a significant difference.

Now is the time for self-inventory. Exactly what is stealing your dream? And what can you do to change your routine to bring you closer to the finish line? Who can you be accountable to?—a person who will help you stay on track.

ERRATIC EMOTIONS

When "discipline" is mentioned, many cringe because it is a word they despise? Why? Because it challenges them to change directions and exercise self-restraint.

Since personal discipline has so much to do with fulfilling our calling, why do so many people struggle with this? The answer is that we don't like to take orders. We prefer to:

- Do *what* we want
- Do it *when* we want
- Do it *how* we want

————— ❧ —————

If left to our feelings, there is no telling where we would end up.

Emotions are erratic and unreliable. For example, when we receive bad news we tend to react with basic negative instincts rather than being thoughtful or logical. However, when discipline is the forerunner, emotions no longer have the ability to lead.

God is not concerned with our action, but with our reaction. A thought-out response, measured, shaken and stirred, is a cocktail more potent than a mixed up concoction of emotions.

Discipline will always do what it is committed to—regardless of how your feelings are responding at the time.

TAKE CHARGE OF YOU

If you are reading this book because of the title on the front cover, you are ready to dare to be different —to step out of the comfort zone in which you have found security for so long. I believe you are being prepared for a major change. Not to be average or even "good," but *great!*

———————— 🕊 ————————

Not one life reaches its potential until it is determined, dedicated, and disciplined.

William Penn, an early champion of U.S. democracy, said, "No man is fit to command another that cannot command himself."

"PROGRESSIVE" TRAINING

Discipline is often associated to legalism, but it is

exactly what is needed to kick-start our dash for the finish line. It is meant to spur you to action, regardless of your emotional state.

Our self-discipline resembles a muscle; the more you train it the stronger it becomes, and without exercise it grows weak and could atrophy.

There are different levels involved. When you first visit a health club they give you an initial workout to measure how much your body can handle.

"Progressive" training means once you succeed in the basics you move to the next step—because if you keep working out with the same weights or resistance, you won't build strength.

Of course, you don't want to overextend yourself when you start on a regimen of self-discipline. If you try to change your entire life too quickly by setting unrealistic goals, you are headed for failure. It's like going for a hundred-pound bench press before you've mastered forty. Your muscles just can't take it.

Eventually, however, your stamina increases and your capacity expands.

THE PATH TO PURE JOY

Point out a person who avoids hard work and I'll show you someone who has yet to find their purpose. Because an individual with direction turns labor into love, and pain into strength. The day will come when their self-submission becomes pure joy.

Paul applied the very same principle to his own ministry when he wrote, *"But I discipline my body and bring it into subjection, lest, when I have preached to others, I myself should become disqualified"* (1 Corinthians 9:27).

A SPECIAL TREASURE

Don't be embarrassed to start. If you lack sufficient self-control, begin by using what little you have. And avoid the trap of comparing yourself with others. It will only result in feelings of inferiority.

When you condition yourself to do what is difficult, you enter into a new realm of positive results.

It's like finding the key to a special treasure. *"For God did not give us a spirit of timidity, but a spirit of power, of love and of self-discipline"* (2 Timothy 1:7 NIV).

I remember studying the lives of people such as Teresa of Avila. This 16th century Spanish nun spent years in self-reflection, inner contemplation, and being absolutely yielded to God. Her spiritual subjection was as real to her as breathing.

Do you know what it means to be pushed to the point where you are stretched to your outer limits, and perhaps even beyond? This is where character development kicks in.

George Washington, when he was commander-in-chief of the American revolutionary forces, observed, "Nothing is more harmful to the service, than the neglect of discipline; for that discipline, more than numbers, gives one army superiority over another."

ACCEPT THE CHALLENGE

When I worked in the personnel business, I was told it would be very beneficial if I would learn to speak the Mandarin language, widely spoken in China.

A few of my friends warned, "Shaneen, that's too tough. You'll never be able to do it."

Their doubts became a challenge, and today I can communicate in Mandarin.

Perhaps you can recall the last time someone said, "You can't."

How did you respond? I hope you quoted the words of the apostle Paul: *"I can do all things through Christ who strengthens me"* (Philippians 4:13).

You not only can, you *will!*

TEN

DARE TO TAKE CHARGE OF YOUR FINANCES

*For every man to whom God has given
riches and wealth, and given him power to
eat of it, to receive his heritage and rejoice
in his labor—this is the gift of God.*

—ECCLESIASTES 5:19

*M*oney is a touchy subject—especially for many Christians. Somehow, we've been led to feel guilty for having too many earthly possessions.

I remember when I was working in property sales and the company gave me a new car to drive; not just an ordinary vehicle, but a sports convertible, plus a mobile phone—which was still a novelty at the time.

In those days I was the youth leader in our church. The first Friday night after receiving the car, I decided to park it as far away from the church as possible—so no one could see my secret possession.

After the youth service, I thought I could leave without anyone following me, but the young people wanted to walk me to my car and have a chat. As I arrived at the car park, about eight youth were still with me; they just couldn't stop talking. I was reluctant to approach my car or even stand near it.

It was getting late, and one young man piped up, "I guess you should be going."

That hot summer evening, I had no choice but to walk to my new convertible and flick the lock open. They looked at me and exclaimed, "Wow! Is that your car? When did you get it?"

Sheepishly, I explained it was a gift from my company. They shouted, "Can we have a ride? Please take the top down!"

I thought, "Okay, let's go girl!" I had to face the truth that this was God's blessing and I didn't need to make excuses for driving such a stylish automobile.

YOUR "GARDEN"

In truth, the Lord wants His children to be blessed, but He also expects us to work for what we receive. In the beginning, *"the Lord God took the man and put him in the garden of Eden to tend and keep it"* (Genesis 2:15).

God placed Adam in the workplace He provided, then gave him the skills to cultivate the soil and do what was necessary to produce crops.

Today, the Lord has also given you a "garden"—the field in which you work. In addition, He has equipped you with the talent and tools to perform whatever is required. Then, in exchange for your efforts, you receive a monetary reward.

Now comes the real test. How do you handle the financial resources you have earned?

———————❧———————

Suppose today you receive your first paycheck. What will you do? Spend it? Or invest the funds wisely and see them grow?

GIVE TO RECEIVE?

In God's economy, there is another requirement —giving. Jesus said, *"Give, and it will be given to you: good measure, pressed down, shaken together, and running over will be put into your bosom. For with*

97

*the same measure that you use, it will be measured
back to you"* (Luke 6:38).

Some ask, "Why do we have to give to receive?
Isn't giving by itself enough?"

The answer is found in the biblical principle that
the law of giving includes receiving. It goes back to
Genesis 8:22: *"While the earth remains, seedtime and
harvest, cold and heat, winter and summer, and day
and night shall not cease."*

————— ❧ —————

**As long as we are on this planet, the
duty to sow and reap will continue. Yet,
we are given the choice to either
obey or reject this principle.**

Tithing, giving one-tenth of what flows through
our hands back to God, it not an option, but a
command of the Almighty. After all, it's not our
money to begin with; we have only been asked to be
stewards of what rightly belongs to Him. Let me
encourage you to read and study Deuteronomy 14:22-
23, Malachi 3:10, and Hebrews 7:1-2.

A PERSONAL TEST

I remember giving a cool new laptop to a person in ministry who was in desperate need of one. Shortly thereafter, mine broke down completely. At this point I was waiting for the Lord to touch someone who would bless me with a new computer—thinking, "Well, I have sown, perhaps now I will reap."

It didn't happen. When I look back, I gave with rejoicing, but then I was about to lose the joy because I didn't receive my wish.

There are times when we are tested by God to see if we will give when He tells us to—regardless. As I learned, this is how He sets the stage to bless us later with more than we can ask or think.

WATCH THOSE WEEDS!

Reaping a harvest requires diligent attention. In the real world, if you neglect your paperwork, things will soon pile up and become such a mess you won't know where to begin. It's like a garden. If we leave it untended, the weeds will grow stronger than the plants and our potential harvest will be in jeopardy.

Here's the process: (1) perform your task, (2) receive your wages, and (3) sow your seed in faith.

Then, as you care for your crops, watch how they will multiply.

I dare you to tend to your work with a giving attitude and watch what happens.

SOWING WHEN TIMES ARE BLEAK

In times of famine, whether the lack is food or finances, God asks you to sow. In Bible times, Isaac was pressured by the community to give up farming, leave his land, and move on. But instead, he decided to obey the Almighty.

Scripture records that during a great drought according to God's command, *"Isaac sowed in that land, and reaped in the same year a hundredfold; and the Lord blessed him. The man began to prosper, and continued prospering until he became very prosperous; for he had possessions of flocks and possessions of herds and a great number of servants. So the Philistines envied him"* (Genesis 26:12-14).

***Sowing—it's God's proven way
of bringing abundance.***

The Lord may allow you to have funds at certain times for a reason. For example, during seasons of recession or depression when the markets are down—there are amazing opportunities to use the money you have invested and purchase property for a fraction of its original cost.

Think of Joseph when he became governor of Egypt. By being wise and listening to God, he saved the grain during the days of plenty and was able to bless many during the days of famine (Genesis 41:47-49).

WHY MONEY?

To some, money is a dirty and sinful word. To others it's the god they worship. Sure, we need monetary funds to meet our needs, but there is often much stress associated with this one topic.

It is vital to understand that money in and of itself is not wicked. According to the Word, it's the *love* of money which is the root of all evil (1 Timothy 6:10).

I don't believe God is against us having wealth—as long as we don't allow wealth to have us!

- Money is used for saving
- Money is used for investing and multiplying

- Money is used for our safety
- Money is used to provide for our family
- Money is used to bless others
- Money is used to preach the Gospel

A vision requires a great deal in terms of finances and the Lord entrusts the funds to us when He examines our hearts and sees we are worthy.

God has designed money for our use, but having the right relationship with it is vital. If funds are not handled according to the Word we will face a multitude of problems.

THE TWO MASTERS

Jesus addressed the subject of money in sixteen out of His thirty-eight parables. In fact, one of every seven verses in the first three Gospels deals in some way with finances.

Perhaps Jesus talked about money more than any topic other than the Kingdom of God because He knows how easily riches can become a god. The Son of God declared, *"No one can serve two masters. Either he will hate the one and love the other, or he will be devoted to the one and despise the other. You cannot serve both God and Money"* (Matthew 6:21 NIV).

Since money is a tool God has given us, how effectively we use this commodity impacts everything we do.

───────── ❧ ─────────

The principles in the Bible are given so we can unblock the pipeline of God's resources.

I truly believe that when you love the Lord with all your heart, do everything within your power to obey His commands, and seek His Kingdom and righteousness first, *"all these things shall be added to you"* (Matthew 6:33).

THE DARING GIVER

One of my friends who had a thriving shoe business decided to sell the entire enterprise and give the profits to a charity. His associates questioned his decision, saying, "You've worked so hard. Why are you doing this?"

His response was, "If I don't, I will never have another successful company." And he added, "Through this principle of giving I have built and maintained my successful business ventures."

103

Years later, his wife became a very successful artist and she too learned to follow in the footprints of her husband.

I challenge you to give even more than the ten percent God requires. The daring giver will see the abundance of the harvest.

BE FAITHFUL WITH LITTLE

In the Parable of the Talents, the servant who doubled his master's money was told, *"Well done, good and faithful servant; you were faithful over a few things, I will make you ruler over many things. Enter into the joy of your lord"* (Matthew:25:21).

In the heart of London, I was privileged to be invited to a small gathering where we heard the marvelous testimony of Dr. Roy Harthern who was miraculously healed of cancer. Tears flowed down his cheeks as he spoke—and I cried with him as I listened to this tall, slim, older gentleman who had been told, "You have only 48 hours to live."

But God, the Great Physician, had other plans!

At the end of the meeting I had a chance to speak with Dr. Harthern and during our conversation I asked him, "How can I really be used by the Lord?"

He confidently replied, "Be faithful with the little

God has given you and He will trust you with much."

I had always thought this concept referred only to money, but now I realize it covers a much broader scope.

——————— ✌ ———————

We often lose the big picture of our dreams because we have not dealt with the small things that hinder us from entering into the greatness of God's calling.

Are there actions you are ignoring because they may seem insignificant? What comes to mind?

I once saw a motto on the wall of a British Post Office that read: "Be careful with the pennies and the pounds will look after you."

How true!

COUNTING THE COST

Examine the project you are about to launch and plan every step you will need to take in order to succeed. Be realistic and assess the downside.

Sometime it's not easy to have a financial cushion in case things go wrong, but to avoid major delays and pitfalls, plan for a monetary squeeze.

Yes, we have faith, but if it doesn't mirror Kingdom principles there will be disappointments (Proverbs 3:5).

There is a profound lesson found in this passage of Scripture:

> *For which of you, intending to build a tower, does not sit down first and count the cost, whether he has enough to finish it—lest, after he has laid the foundation, and is not able to finish, all who see it begin to mock him, saying, "This man began to build and was not able to finish"? Or what king, going to make war against another king, does not sit down first and consider whether he is able with ten thousand to meet him who comes against him with twenty thousand? Or else, while the other is still a great way off, he sends a delegation and asks conditions of peace. So likewise, whoever of you does not forsake all that he has cannot be My disciple* (Luke 14:28-33).

WHO DO YOUR TRUST?

The principles involved in any undertaking

include (1) calculating the cost, (2) laying the foundation on solid ground (the Word of God), and (3) seeking godly counsel.

It is always smart to have trusted advisors. When you face those sticky moments, people with wise judgement, talent, who are experts in specific areas, and have broad experience will prove invaluable. But remember, it is you who will always have to make the final decision, and must live with the consequences.

———————— ❧ ————————

When you become proficient at whatever project you undertake, people will love dealing with you.

The Lord also expects us to be honorable and fair.

A Chinese man once said, "In business my principle of success is to be fair. When I have told clients they were paying too much, they trusted me and I have made more money in the long run."

King Solomon stated, *"Honest weights and scales are the Lord's; all the weights in the bag are His work"* (Proverbs 16.11).

REASONS FOR LACK

You fight traffic, toil hard all day, and even bring work home—attempting to juggle career aspirations alongside family commitments.

In addition, the daunting task of managing your financial affairs can often feel like a hammer just hit you on the head!

On this emotional roller coaster, you rush out to the shops and pay with a credit card, leaving the worry of debt for another time.

I believe there are many reasons for living in lack, including:

1. Not giving
2. Not saving
3. Not investing
4. A poverty mindset
5. Lack of financial knowledge
6. Being an emotional shopper
7. Not comprehending the tyranny of debt
8. Greed
9. Wrong motives

BREAKING THE CYCLE

Debt has a tendency to kill dreams, but you can resurrect them back to life by applying the biblical principle: *"Let no debt remain outstanding, except the continuing debt to love one another"* (Romans 13.8 NIV).

The "plastic" lifestyle of credit cards is deception disguised in the promise that you can have it all NOW. This instant greed, which is robbing so many believers, is a lie of Satan that seeks to keep Christians drowning in debt, preventing them from freely giving to the spreading of the Gospel.

In both the United States and Great Britain the amount of credit card debt continues to rise, and personal bankruptcies have been soaring.

So what is the answer to breaking the cycle of debt? Since *"the borrower is servant to the lender" (Proverbs 22.7)*, we must pursue the path where we *"owe no man anything"* (Romans 13:8 KJV).

———— ❧ ————

The buy-now-pay-later theory is sucking millions into debt and loss of vision.

I interviewed a young Oxford University graduate on the subject of money. His research proved that without us having financial liabilities the banks could not survive—thus they have a vested interest in seeing us owing rather than owning.

FIFTEEN STEPS

How do we dare to be debt free? First, realize that not all debt is a sin, but it surely is not the wisest way to live. In a recent study, 71% of Americans say owing money is making their home life unhappy.

We need to implement these fifteen steps:

1. Wait to buy until you have the cash. By the time you pay off the interest on a credit card purchase, you could have paid cash for three items of similar cost.

2. When taking money out of a bank cash point or ATM machine, take the least amount possible. Controlling this habit will save you a considerable amount. Just because it's available doesn't mean you need to spend it!

3. Be accountable. My husband and I spoke at a church where the members were wallowing in such debt we encouraged them to form "accountability groups" within the congregation with the goal of either greatly reducing or paying off what they owed. A few months later, we received a report that many had already totally conquered their debt.

4. Don't risk your own credit by signing for another person's obligations (Proverbs 22.26-27).

5. Count the cost when building your business and seek advice of others who are well-informed. The Bible tells us, *"In a multitude of counselors there is safety"* (Proverbs 24:6).

6. Stop shopping for what you don't need.

7. Count the pennies.

8. Pay your bills and taxes promptly. I asked a prominent businessman, "What's your number

one rule for a successful enterprise." He replied, "Take care of your obligations quickly."

10. Discipline yourselves to live thirty percent below your means. Most people live way beyond what they can afford. Experts say it takes about five years for credit to catch up with you. When you borrow your spending tomorrow's money.

11. Always know the true state of your finances. God says, *"My people are destroyed for lack of knowledge"* Hosea 4:6).

12. Watch out for greed? This is what gets you caught in the web of debt.

13. Make sure you don't fall into the trap of only giving to receive. We give because we love the Lord first and foremost—and to see the Gospel of Christ preached. The benefits are God's business.

14. Take a scissors to your credit cards.

15. Ask yourself, "How badly do I want to get out of debt?" Then pay the price and do it.

Right now, I dare you to dig yourself out of the pit of indebtedness—and *stay* out. You don't need the pain and pressure of being its slave. The few moments of self-gratification are not worth the ride.

———————⟡———————

Satan loves to abuse this particular area of our lives because he knows the power of money and the bondage of debt.

Refuse to give the devil one more foothold (Ephesians 4:27).

NO COMPROMISE

During one period, I did not have any credit cards for two years. I remember the pinch I used to feel when paying cash—but it taught me to appreciate the true value of money.

In the process I began to see miracles in my finances and my bank account was growing in ways I had never experienced.

113

Remain in the Word of God regardless of how tough the pressures of finances may be. Do not compromise the principles of Scripture.

Stock markets, business fortunes, home values, and our bank balances are always going to fluctuate, but rest in the fact that God's principles can never be moved or changed. It is the solid, sure foundation that will take you and your finances through the shaky times of life.

ELEVEN

DARE TO STAY FOCUSED

Let your eyes look straight ahead.
−PROVERBS 4:25

I can't count the number of times I've heard people complain, "I'm so frustrated. I try to stay focused on my objective, but it seems there is always something distracting me."

Frustration leads to disappointment and causes individuals to become dissatisfied or unfulfilled. If not dealt with, they will spend their final years wondering what could have been.

Let's face the facts: over ninety percent fail to realize their dream—and this includes well intentioned Christians. Why? It's certainly not because God doesn't want them to. They have not

115

dared to zero in on their ultimate purpose and take action.

If you find yourself trapped in the "frustrated" category, confront and deal with it immediately. Do not place the blame on others.

———— ❧ ————

Take the responsibility to do something about your "dream drainers." If you stop feeding them, they will die.

You must decide to take whatever steps are necessary to get your life back on track. In the insightful words of author Jack Dixon, "If you focus on results, you will never change. If you focus on change, you will get results."

Identify what is derailing you. Make the required adjustments and don't let anything pull you away from what God has called you to be. The One who loves you beyond measure can turn your frustrations into satisfactions.

SPIRITUAL VISION

Here is what the noted clergyman A. W. Tozer wrote: "When we come before the throne of God, we are not going to be able to say to God, 'God, I would have liked on earth to have reached, to have possessed, to have known such a place, such a condition, such a level of faith or ministry...' or whatever it is. We will not be able to say that because God will turn around and say, 'Child, I gave you everything you needed to fulfill everything you've seen.'"

Tozer is talking about spiritual vision.

———— ❦ ————

The Lord does not demand of us anything He has not shown us.

What has God revealed to you lately? If your answer is "nothing," immediately put this book down and begin to pray for Him to impart the vision He has for you. When He does, cling to it as if it were the last life raft on a sinking vessel. Keep it close to your heart and constantly in your thoughts.

117

NEVER AGAIN

The next time you are feeling "down" or burdened with doubts, start making commitments to yourself and to the Lord.

In many situations, I turn to these Scriptures compiled by an unknown author—and often quote them out loud. They inspire and give me the assurance that no matter how bleak the situation, God has the perfect answer:

Go ahead and declare:

- NEVER AGAIN will I confess or focus on "I can't," because the Word says: *"I can do all things through Christ who strengthens me."* (Philippians 4:13).

- NEVER AGAIN will I confess or focus on fear, because the Word says: *"God has not given [me] a spirit of fear, but of power and of love and of a sound mind"* (2 Timothy 1:7).

- NEVER AGAIN will I confess or focus on doubt

and a lack of faith, because the Word says: *"God has dealt to each one [every person] a measure of faith"* (Romans 12:3).

- NEVER AGAIN will I confess or focus on weakness, because the Word says: *"The Lord is the strength of my life"* (Psalm 27:1) and *"The people who know their God shall be strong, and carry out great exploits"* (Daniel 11:32).

- NEVER AGAIN will I confess or focus on the supremacy of Satan over my life, because the Word says: *"Greater is he that is in [me], than he that is in the world"* (1 John 4:4 KJV).

- NEVER AGAIN will I confess or focus on defeat, because the Word says: *"God...always leads [me] to triumph in Christ"* (2 Corinthians 2:14).

- NEVER AGAIN will I confess or focus on a lack of wisdom, because the Word says: *"Christ Jesus...became for [me] wisdom from God"* (1 Corinthians 1:30) and *"If any of you lacks*

119

wisdom, let him ask of God, who gives to all liberally, and it will be given to him" (James 1:5).

- NEVER AGAIN will I confess or focus on sickness, because the Word says: *"By His stripes [I am] healed"* (Isaiah 53:5) and Jesus *"Himself took [my] infirmities and bore [my] sickness"* (Matthew 8:17).

- NEVER AGAIN will I confess or focus on bondage, because the Word says: *"Where the Spirit of the Lord is, there is liberty"* (2 Corinthians 3:17) and *"[My] body is the temple of the Holy Spirit who is in [me]"* (1 Corinthians 6:19).

- NEVER AGAIN will I confess or focus on worries and frustration, because the Word says: I am *"Casting all [my] cares upon Him, for He cares for [me]"* (1 Peter 5:7).

- NEVER AGAIN will I confess or focus on

condemnation, because the Word says: *"There is...now no condemnation to those who are in Christ Jesus"* (Romans 8:1). I am in Christ, so therefore I am free from condemnation!

- NEVER AGAIN will I confess or focus on loneliness, because Jesus said: *"I am with you always, even to the end of the age [forever]"* (Matthew 28:20) and *"I will never leave you nor forsake you"* (Hebrews 13:5).

- NEVER AGAIN will I confess or focus on curses or bad luck, because the Word says: *"Christ has redeemed [me] from the curse of the law, having become a curse for [me]...that the blessings of Abraham might come upon the Gentiles [that's me] in Christ Jesus, that [I] might receive the promise of the Spirit through faith"* (Galatians 3:13-14).

- NEVER AGAIN will I confess or focus on discontentment, because the Word says: *"I have learned in whatever state [circumstance] I am, to be content"* (Philippians 4:11).

121

- NEVER AGAIN will I confess or focus on unworthiness, because the Word says: *"He made Him who knew no sin to be sin for [me], that [I] might become the righteousness of God in Him"* (2 Corinthians 5:21).

- NEVER AGAIN will I confess or focus on confusion, because the Word says: *"God is not the author of confusion but of peace"* (1 Corinthians 14:33) and *"We have received, not the spirit of the world, but the Spirit who is from God, that we might know the things that have been freely given to us by God"* (1 Corinthians 2:12).

- NEVER AGAIN will I confess or focus on persecution, because the Word says: *"If God be for us, who can be against us?"* (Romans 8:31).

- NEVER AGAIN will I confess or focus on the domination of sin over my life, because the Word says: *"The law of the Spirit of life in*

Christ Jesus has made me free from the law of sin and death"(Romans 8:2).

- NEVER AGAIN will I confess or focus on insecurity, because the Word says: *"When you lie down, you will not be afraid; yes, you will lie down and your sleep will be sweet. Do not be afraid of sudden terror, nor of trouble from the wicked when it comes; for the Lord will be your confidence, and will keep your foot from being caught"*(Proverbs 3:24-26).

- NEVER AGAIN will I confess or focus on failure, because the Word says: *"In all these things we are more than conquerors through Him who loved us"*(Romans 8:37).

- NEVER AGAIN will I confess or focus on frustration, because the Word says: *"You will keep him in perfect peace, whose mind is stayed on You, because he trusts in You"*(Isaiah 26:3).

- NEVER AGAIN will I confess or focus on fear

of the future, because the Word says: *"'Eye has not seen, nor ear heard, nor have entered into the heart of man the things which God has prepared for those who love Him.' But God has revealed them to us through His Spirit"* (1 Corinthians 2:9-10).

- NEVER AGAIN will I confess or focus on troubles, because Jesus said, *"In the world you will have tribulation; but be of good cheer, I have overcome the world"* (John 16:33).

What About You?

In today's culture of information overload, with so much data to keep track of, we struggle to concentrate on our life's objective. Yet, if we are going to achieve what God has planted within us, there is no alternative but to keep our eyes riveted on the prize!

- Elisha was totally focused: he would not leave the prophet Elijah's side until he received a double portion of his anointing (2 Kings 2:1-9).

- Jesus was totally focused: He said, *"I must preach the kingdom of God...because for this purpose I have been sent"* (Luke 4:43) and *"I must be about My Father's business"* (Luke 2:49).

- The apostle Paul was totally focused: he declared, *"This one thing I do"* (Philippians 3:13).

What about you? Are you ready to bid farewell to frustration? You can by blocking out the tumult and diversions all around you and keeping your mind, heart and soul pointing toward the direction of your God-given dream.

TWELVE

DARE TO STEP INTO GREATNESS

*You shall increase my greatness,
and comfort me on every side.*

−PSALM 71:21

*N*ow it's your turn!

As you have read these pages, I pray you understand how you are valued by God. You were created in His likeness and are essential to His plan on earth. Your heavenly Father also planted the seeds of greatness in you—which He expects to blossom and grow.

This will only happen if you challenge yourself to move from the natural to the *supernatural*, from the common to the uncommon, from the ordinary to the *extraordinary*.

In other words you must dare yourself to change.

127

Dare to be Humble

Most people recognize humility for what it's *not*. For example, a humble person isn't conceited, haughty, or consumed with arrogance.

And we identify these characteristics quickly when we see them demonstrated—as when the proud Pharisee stood in the temple and prayed, *"God, I thank You that I am not like other men"* (Luke 18:11).

This religious man was filled with self-importance in his own eyes, but not in the Lord's sight. I'm sure those around him could see right through his hypocrisy.

What did Jesus have to say on the subject? *"Everyone who exalts himself will be humbled, and he who humbles himself will be exalted"* (Luke 18:14).

The contrite person, to quote the apostle Paul, does not *"think of himself more highly than he ought to think"* (Romans 12:3).

In fact, just the opposite, he is gracious and kind, never seeking special favors to gain an advantage over others.

Dare to Wait

My husband is involved in an enterprise where on occasion he has to wait for rather long periods for others to make decisions. More than once I have impatiently commented, "Martin, why don't you make a call or do something?"

He will calmly reply, "The timing's not right."

The Bible tells us there is a time to sow and a time to reap (Ecclesiastes 3), but the actions are never done simultaneously. As the psalmist wrote, *"The eyes of all look expectantly to You, and You give them their food in due season"* (Psalm 145:15). And we read, *"Let us not grow weary while doing good, for in due season we shall reap if we do not lose heart"* (Galatians 6:9).

Start practicing the virtue called patience. David said, *"My soul, wait silently for God alone, for my expectation is from Him"* (Psalm 62:5).

———— ❧ ————

Greatness is not achieved on our schedule, but on the Lord's.

Dare to Seek God's Will

Glance over the titles displayed at a newsstand and

you'll see dozens of magazines promoting health, beauty, sex, fashion and self-improvement. It's not hard to see why the average person finds it so difficult to align their will with the Creator of the earth. Why? Because, we would rather sing, like Frank Sinatra, "I did it my way."

God's Kingdom requires the opposite approach —doing things according to His will.

I love these words penned by evangelist T. L. Osborn:

I am VALUABLE to God and to people because I am created in His class of being.

I am VITAL because God's plan involves me.

MY HERITAGE is to have God's best to enjoy His companionship and to use His wealth and power for the good of myself and others.

I am CREATED for life, love, power, prosperity, success, and dignity.

The SEEDS OF GREATNESS are in me. God never created me to be a nobody, but a real somebody.

I therefore recognize my self-value, that God designed me for His lifestyle and now know that He planned Life's BEST for me as His child.

I shall no longer discredit or demean or destroy what God created in His image and values so much.

I welcome God's friendly voice. He reminds me of my divine origin, of my high purpose, and of His Love-Plan to help me achieve, enjoy and share His best in life.

Reading and rereading these inspiring thoughts will help you to come into agreement with your heavenly Father's will.

Dare to Surrender

There is absolutely no substitute for a life that is totally yielded to the Lord.

To give you an example of what can happen when just one person is completely surrendered, let me share this account which was reported in the Fall 1970 edition of the *Yale (University) Standard.*

In 1904 William Borden graduated from a Chicago high school. As heir to the Borden Dairy estate, he was already a millionaire. For his high school graduation present, his parents gave 16-year-old Borden a trip around the world. As the young man traveled through Asia, the Middle East, and Europe, he felt a growing burden for the world's hurting people. Finally, Bill Borden wrote home about his "desire to be a missionary."

One friend expressed surprise that he was "throwing himself away as a missionary."

In response, Bill wrote two words in the back of his Bible: "No reserves."

Even though young Borden was wealthy, he arrived on the campus of Yale University in 1905 trying to look like just one more freshman. Very quickly, however, Borden's classmates noticed something unusual about him and it wasn't his money. He had surrendered his life totally to Christ, and classmates found him as solid as a rock because of his settled purpose.

During his college years, Bill Borden made one entry in his personal journal that defined what his classmates were seeing in him. That entry said simply: "Say 'no' to self and 'yes' to Jesus."

After lamenting what he viewed as students

and faculty with empty philosophy, moral weakness and sin-ruined lives, during his first semester at Yale, Borden started early morning prayer meetings with a friend. Soon there were three, then four, then more. At the end of the first year, over 150 freshmen were meeting for weekly Bible study and prayer. And by the time he was a senior, one thousand of Yale's 1,300 students were meeting in such groups.

Borden's outreach ministry was not confined to the Yale campus. He cared about widows and orphans and cripples. He rescued drunks from the streets of New Haven. To rehabilitate them, he founded the Yale Hope Mission. At the same time, he served as president of the honor society, Phi Beta Kappa.

Borden's missionary call narrowed to the Muslim Kansu people in China. Once that goal was in sight, Borden never wavered. He also inspired his classmates to consider missionary service.

After receiving his degree he turned down high paying job offers. In his Bible, he wrote two more words: "No retreats."

Borden went on to graduate work at Princeton Seminary in New Jersey. When he finished these studies, he sailed for China. And, because he was hoping to work with Muslims, he stopped first in Egypt to study Arabic. While there, he contracted spinal meningitis. Within a month, 25-year-old William Borden was dead.

When news of his death was cabled back to the U.S., the story was carried by nearly every American newspaper. It was written, "Borden not only gave (away) his wealth, but himself, in a way so joyous and natural that it (seemed) a privilege rather than a sacrifice."

In God's plan, Borden's untimely demise was not a waste. Prior to his death, he had written two more words in his Bible. Underneath the words "No reserves" and "No retreats," he had written: "No regrets."

Oh, for a new generation of William Bordens who will shake this world!

Dare to Fulfill God's Vision

Since time cannot be recaptured, there will never

be another today. One thing is clear, when God gives you a purpose, you will suddenly be able to accomplish far more in the same number of hours than ever before. I am not referring to simply doing good works. Rather, being involved in what we are truly called to do here on earth.

How will you know if you are fulfilling God's calling for your life? Answer these questions:

- Is there "fruit"—are you seeing results from your efforts?
- Do you enjoy your daily activities?
- Do you feel a sense of urgency, or a passion for your endeavors?

If your answer is "no," you are just filling in time, keeping yourself busy, and fitting in with those around you. You will know you are passionate in your mission because of the harvest it will eventually produce —regardless of how long it takes.

It's like planting bamboo. You may not see any growth for a considerable time, then suddenly the bamboo shoots up six feet!

Even as you are reading this book, God can plant

His vision within you and your reason for being will spring to life. Even more, clarity will become your friend.

Let me add this warning: you can also have a burning desire for the wrong objective. As James writes, *"You ask and do not receive, because you ask amiss"* (James 4:3).

———— ✍ ————

Always check your thoughts and inner-drives with the Lord and allow Him to work as your Partner.

Take plenty of time for personal inventory and self-evaluation.

This shouldn't take too long, but it does require your willingness to cooperate with the Holy Spirit. One of the vital power principles of Christian living is activated when you finally reach the point where your will becomes His will.

Dare to be Sold Out

Many wish and hope to accomplish lofty goals and

noble objectives, but few are willing to pay the price—they are even afraid to look at the tag!

The great "zero to hero" stories have one common denominator. The winners keep pressing forward and do whatever it takes to claim the prize.

During a graduation speech at England's famed Harrow School in 1941, Winston Churchill gave one of the shortest, but perhaps the most powerful addresses in history. He simply told his audience: "Never, never, never, never give in."

When nothing else matters, you are finally ready to receive God's best.

As I mentioned in chapter one, as a young girl I was inspired by the American evangelist Kathryn Kuhlman. When this incredible woman was interviewed by the press, she was often asked, "Kathryn, you have been divorced, How have you coped with this in your ministry?"

Her response was, "That Kathryn Kulhman died a long time ago." In other words, her past was buried.

She made a decision to never look back, and she lived by the words of Paul: *"I press toward the goal for the prize of the upward call of God in Christ Jesus"* (Philippians 3:14).

————— 🙦 —————

Miss Kuhlman said many times, "You don't know the price I have paid for this calling."

What does SOLD OUT mean to you? To a store owner it might stand for bare shelves and high profits. However, to me it conveys being dedicated, transferred, and surrendered completely.

THE ULTIMATE PRICE

The greatest story ever told is summarized in these words found in John 3:16: *"For God so loved the world that He gave His only begotten Son, that whoever believes in Him should not perish but have everlasting life."*

Your salvation came as the result of a sold out life. Jesus paid the ultimate price when your sins were nailed to the cross and His blood provided cleansing for your heart. All that is required to receive God's redemption and to enter into the great life He offers is to accept this priceless gift by faith.

Please repeat this prayer with me.

Lord, I accept You into my life. Forgive me of my sins and accept me as Your child. Thank You, Lord, for saving me now. I promise to pray, read Your Word, and strive to become the best at what You call me to be. I will accomplish your perfect will in my life.

Amen.

By praying this prayer you have dared to step into greatness!

NOTES

_____

_____

_____

_____

_____

_____

_____

_____

_____

_____

_____

_____

_____

_____

_____

_____

For a Complete List of
Media Resources or to
Schedule the Author for
Speaking Engagements,
Contact:

Shaneen Clarke
P.O. Box 31688
South Kensington
London, UK SW7 2WZ

Phone: 44- (0) 7852 137066
Internet: www.shaneenclark.org